MW01397168

THIS JOURNAL BELONGS TO

_____

_____ / _____
DATE STARTED   DATE COMPLETED

Word First
WOMEN

HOW TO USE THIS JOURNAL

THIS JOURNAL UTILIZES A SIMPLE BIBLE STUDY METHOD TO HELP YOU INTERACT WITH GOD'S WORD EACH DAY. THE INFORMATION BELOW WILL WALK YOU THROUGH HOW TO DIG DEEP INTO SCRIPTURE AND TO REFLECT UPON HOW YOU CAN APPLY IT TO YOUR LIFE. AFTER ALL, IT ISN'T ENOUGH TO JUST READ GOD'S WORD - WE MUST LET IT TRANSFORM US FROM THE INSIDE OUT!

SCRIPTURE

God's Word speaks to every situation or challenge that we will ever face. How comforting to know that we can get our guidance directly from the One who knows and created all things! We can approach his Word with confidence, knowing that every word is flawless and true. Ask God to speak to you through his Scriptures and to reveal his heart to you. We recommend reading the selected Scripture several times before you begin!

OBSERVE

Use this section to record anything that stands out to you or that the Lord has put on your heart. Underline, highlight and write notes on the verse itself. Ask yourself: *What is the verse/passage saying? What stood out and why? What words or concepts do I not understand? (Tip: Look them up!) What did I learn about myself? More importantly, what did I learn about God?* For further context, read the full chapter or passage in your Bible.

TRANSFORM

You've read God's Word. You've analyzed it, researched things you didn't understand and asked yourself important questions about yourself and God. Now, what will you do with that information? Ask yourself: *How can I apply what I just learned to my life today? What practical steps can I take to apply these truths to my life? How will my life change because of this?*

SEEK

End in a time of seeking God in prayer. There is no right or wrong way to pray. Your words don't need to be fancy or eloquent - the Lord knows your heart and longs to communicate with you no matter what. Thank him for his Word and ask him to help you store up and apply the things that you have learned **so that you may be transformed**!

SAMPLE

Let the (morning) bring me word of your (unfailing) love, for I have put my trust in you. (Show me) the way I should go, for to you I entrust my life.

Psalm 143:8

OBSERVE

Unfailing:
without error or fault
reliable/constant.

He will lead if you ask!

His love will never fail me — why wouldn't I trust Him?

TRANSFORM

Make a habit of meeting with God first thing in the morning! This shows what my priority is and fixes my eyes on Him. There is no better way to start my day!

Trust God's plan over my plan!!!

SEEK

Lord — Thank you for your unfailing love! Forgive me for trying to control my life instead of trusting you, for I know that your plan is always best. Give me the discipline and commitment to meet with you each morning — so that you would be able to guide me each day. Amen.

MY PEACE I GIVE YOU

Anxiety hits us from all directions - whether it be our jobs, our children, our health, our finances or anything else that causes us to fear the future. For some, worry is circumstantial, coming and going in waves in a seemingly harmless way. For others, the effects of anxiety are heavier, taking a significant toll both emotionally and physically. However, regardless of the *weight* of our worry, the *root* of our worry remains the same - fixing our eyes on our *problems*, rather than our *God*.

Over the next thirty days, you'll dive into the Scriptures to discover what God says about worry and anxiety, how he calls us to handle it and how we can leave it all behind for a life of true peace and freedom.

PEACE I LEAVE WITH YOU; MY PEACE I GIVE YOU. I DO NOT GIVE TO YOU AS THE WORLD GIVES. DO NOT LET YOUR HEARTS BE TROUBLED AND DO NOT BE AFRAID.

JOHN 14:27

SEEK

ME

FIRST

THE ONLY TRUE AND LASTING ANTIDOTE FOR OUR ANXIETY IS JESUS. IT IS WHEN WE CHOOSE TO FIX OUR EYES FULLY ON HIM, THAT WE CAN EXPERIENCE PEACE THAT SURPASSES ALL UNDERSTANDING.

"Therefore I tell you, do not worry about your life, what you will eat; or about your body, what you will wear. For life is more than food, and the body more than clothes. Consider the ravens: They do not sow or reap, they have no storeroom or barn; yet God feeds them. And how much more valuable you are than birds! Who of you by worrying can add a single hour to your life? Since you cannot do this very little thing, why do you worry about the rest?

"Consider how the wild flowers grow. They do not labor or spin. Yet I tell you, not even Solomon in all his splendor was dressed like one of these. If that is how God clothes the grass of the field, which is here today, and tomorrow is thrown into the fire, how much more will he clothe you—you of little faith! And do not set your heart on what you will eat or drink; do not worry about it. For the pagan world runs after all such things, and your Father knows that you need them. But seek his kingdom, and these things will be given to you as well.

Luke 12:22-31

PREPARE

YOUR

HEART

TAKE SOME TIME TO PRAYERFULLY

CONSIDER THE ANXIETIES THAT YOU

FACE AND HUMBLY LAY THEM

AT THE FEET OF JESUS TODAY.

LORD, I AM OFTEN ANXIOUS ABOUT

I AM LAYING THESE THINGS AT YOUR FEET BECAUSE

I PRAY THIS STUDY HELPS ME

SO YOU HAVE NOT RECEIVED A SPIRIT THAT MAKES YOU FEARFUL SLAVES. INSTEAD, YOU RECEIVED GOD'S SPIRIT WHEN HE ADOPTED YOU AS HIS OWN CHILDREN.

―

Romans 8:15

TRUTH NO. 1

Do not be anxious about anything, but in every situation, by prayer and petition, with thanksgiving, present your requests to God. And the peace of God, which transcends all understanding, will guard your hearts and your minds in Christ Jesus.

Philippians 4:6-7

OBSERVE

TRANSFORM

SEEK

TRUTH NO. 2

So we say with confidence, "The Lord is my helper;
I will not be afraid. What can mere mortals do to me?"

Hebrews 13:6

OBSERVE

TRANSFORM

SEEK

TRUTH NO. 3

**You will keep in perfect peace
those whose minds are steadfast,
because they trust in you.**

Isaiah 26:3

OBSERVE

TRANSFORM

SEEK

TRUTH NO. 4

Look at the birds of the air; they do not sow or reap or store away in barns, and yet your heavenly Father feeds them. Are you not much more valuable than they? Can any one of you by worrying add a single hour to your life?

Matthew 6:26-27

OBSERVE

TRANSFORM

SEEK

I WILL REFRESH

THE WEARY

AND SATISFY

THE FAINT.

―

Jeremiah 31:25

TRUTH NO. 5

**When anxiety was great within me,
your consolation brought me joy.**

Psalm 94:19

OBSERVE

TRANSFORM

SEEK

TRUTH NO. 6

May the God of hope fill you with all joy and peace as you trust in him, so that you may overflow with hope by the power of the Holy Spirit.

Romans 15:13

OBSERVE

TRANSFORM

SEEK

TRUTH NO. 7

Come to me, all you who are weary and burdened, and I will give you rest. Take my yoke upon you and learn from me, for I am gentle and humble in heart, and you will find rest for your souls.

Matthew 11:28-29

OBSERVE

TRANSFORM

SEEK

TRUTH NO. 8

**For God has not given us a spirit of fear,
but of power and of love and of a sound mind.**

2 Timothy 1:7

OBSERVE

_____
_____
_____
_____
_____
_____
_____

TRANSFORM

_____
_____
_____
_____
_____
_____
_____

SEEK

_____
_____
_____
_____
_____
_____
_____

AND HE SAID,

"MY PRESENCE SHALL

GO WITH YOU,

AND I WILL

GIVE YOU REST.

———

Exodus 33:14

TRUTH NO. 9

For I know the plans I have for you," declares the Lord, "plans to prosper you and not to harm you, plans to give you hope and a future.

Jeremiah 29:11

OBSERVE

TRANSFORM

SEEK

TRUTH NO. 10

Therefore do not worry about tomorrow, for tomorrow will worry about itself. Each day has enough trouble of its own.

Matthew 6:34

OBSERVE

TRANSFORM

SEEK

TRUTH NO. 11

So do not fear, for I am with you; do not be dismayed, for I am your God. I will strengthen you and help you; I will uphold you with my righteous right hand.

Isaiah 41:10

OBSERVE

TRANSFORM

SEEK

TRUTH NO. 12

But those who hope in the Lord will renew their strength. They will soar on wings like eagles; they will run and not grow weary, they will walk and not be faint.

Isaiah 40:31

OBSERVE

TRANSFORM

SEEK

MY FLESH AND MY

HEART MAY FAIL,

BUT GOD IS THE

STRENGTH OF MY

HEART AND MY

PORTION FOREVER.

―

John 15:13

TRUTH NO. 13

Have I not commanded you? Be strong and courageous. Do not be terrified; do not be discouraged, for the Lord your God will be with you wherever you go.

Joshua 1:9

OBSERVE

TRANSFORM

SEEK

TRUTH NO. 14

**Cast your cares on the Lord and he will sustain you;
he will never let the righteous fall.**

Psalm 55:22

OBSERVE

TRANSFORM

SEEK

TRUTH NO. 15

Peace I leave with you; my peace I give you. I do not give to you as the world gives. Do not let your hearts be troubled and do not be afraid.

John 14:27

OBSERVE

_____
_____
_____
_____
_____
_____

TRANSFORM

_____
_____
_____
_____
_____
_____

SEEK

_____
_____
_____
_____
_____
_____

TRUTH NO. 16

**What, then, shall we say in response to these things?
If God is for us, who can be against us?**

Romans 8:31

OBSERVE

TRANSFORM

SEEK

I LIFT UP MY EYES

TO THE MOUNTAINS —

WHERE DOES MY HELP COME

FROM? MY HELP COMES FROM

THE LORD, THE MAKER OF

HEAVEN AND EARTH.

———

Psalm 121:1-2

TRUTH NO. 17

Return to your rest, my soul, for the Lord has been good to you.
Psalm 116:7

OBSERVE

TRANSFORM

SEEK

TRUTH NO. 18

I have told you these things, so that in me you may have peace. In this world you will have trouble. But take heart! I have overcome the world.

John 16:33

OBSERVE

_____
_____
_____
_____
_____
_____

TRANSFORM

_____
_____
_____
_____
_____
_____

SEEK

_____
_____
_____
_____
_____
_____

TRUTH NO. 19

**In peace I will lie down and sleep, for you alone,
Lord, make me dwell in safety.**

Psalm 4:8

OBSERVE

TRANSFORM

SEEK

TRUTH NO. 20

I prayed to the Lord, and he answered me. He freed me from all my fears. Those who look to him for help will be radiant with joy; no shadow of shame will darken their faces.

Psalm 34:4-5

OBSERVE

TRANSFORM

SEEK

I WILL INSTRUCT YOU AND

TEACH YOU IN THE WAY YOU

SHOULD GO; I WILL COUNSEL YOU

WITH MY LOVING EYE ON YOU.

———

Psalm 32:8

TRUTH NO. 21

My soul finds rest in God alone; my salvation comes from him. He alone is my rock and my salvation; he is my fortress, I will never be shaken.

Psalm 62:1-2

OBSERVE

TRANSFORM

SEEK

TRUTH NO. 22

Why are you downcast, O my soul? Why so disturbed within me?
Put your hope in God, for I will yet praise Him, my Savior and my God.

Psalm 42:5

OBSERVE

TRANSFORM

SEEK

TRUTH NO. 23

But now, this is what the Lord says… "Fear not, for I have redeemed you; I have summoned you by name; you are mine."

Isaiah 43:1

OBSERVE

TRANSFORM

SEEK

TRUTH NO. 24

Whoever dwells in the shelter of the Most High will rest in the shadow of the Almighty. I will say of the Lord, "He is my refuge and my fortress, my God, in whom I trust."

Hebrews 12:2

OBSERVE

TRANSFORM

SEEK

GREAT PEACE HAVE

THOSE WHO LOVE

YOUR LAW, AND NOTHING

CAN MAKE THEM STUMBLE.

———

2 Corinthians 4:17

TRUTH NO. 25

So we fix our eyes not on what is seen, but on what is unseen, since what is seen is temporary, but what is unseen is eternal.

2 Corinthians 4:18

OBSERVE

TRANSFORM

SEEK

TRUTH NO. 26

**Whatever you have learned or received or heard from me,
or seen in me — put it into practice. And the God of peace will be with you.**

Philippians 4:9

OBSERVE

TRANSFORM

SEEK

TRUTH NO. 27

And we know that in all things God works for the good of those who love Him, who have been called according to His purpose.

Romans 8:28

OBSERVE

TRANSFORM

SEEK

TRUTH NO. 28

For I am convinced that neither death nor life, neither angels nor demons, neither the present nor the future, nor any powers, neither height nor depth, nor anything else in all creation, will be able to separate us from the love of God that is in Christ Jesus our Lord.

Romans 8:38-39

OBSERVE

TRANSFORM

SEEK

THUS SAYS THE LORD:

"STAND BY THE ROADS,

AND LOOK, AND ASK FOR

THE ANCIENT PATHS,

WHERE THE GOOD WAY IS;

AND WALK IN IT, AND FIND

REST FOR YOUR SOULS.

—

Philippians 1:6

TRUTH NO. 29

The Lord, your God, is in your midst, a warrior who gives victory; he will rejoice over you with gladness, he will renew you in his love; he will exult over you with loud singing.

Zephaniah 3:17

OBSERVE

TRANSFORM

SEEK

TRUTH NO. 30

Now may the Lord of peace himself give you peace at all times and in every way. The Lord be with all of you.

2 Thessalonians 3:16

OBSERVE

....
....
....
....
....
....
....

TRANSFORM

....
....
....
....
....
....

SEEK

....
....
....
....
....
....
....

BLESSED IS THE MAN WHO TRUSTS IN THE LORD, WHOSE TRUST IS THE LORD. HE IS LIKE A TREE PLANTED BY WATER, THAT SENDS OUT ITS ROOTS BY THE STREAM, AND DOES NOT FEAR WHEN HEAT COMES, FOR ITS LEAVES REMAIN GREEN, AND IS NOT ANXIOUS IN THE YEAR OF DROUGHT, FOR IT DOES NOT CEASE TO BEAR FRUIT.

———

Jeremiah 17:7-8

REFLECTION

**Take some time to reflect on the past 30 days.
Use the following questions to prompt your heart and mind.**

> What lies have you believed about anxiety?
> What worries are you choosing to leave at the cross?
> How has God worked in your heart the past 30 days?
> What did you learn about God? About yourself?
> How has your perspective on worry and anxiety changed?
> How will you let these truths transform your life?

SHARE YOUR JOURNEY WITH US!

WORDFIRSTWOMEN@GMAIL.COM

#WORDFIRSTMOMENTS
@WORDFIRSTWOMEN

©2020 Word First Women. All rights reserved. All contents of this journal are copyrighted and cannot be copied or reproduced for any purpose without prior written permission of the author, except in the case of brief quotations embodied in critical reviews and certain other non-commercial uses permitted by copyright law.

Scriptures taken from the Holy Bible, New International Version®, NIV®. Copyright © 1973, 1978, 1984, 2011 by Biblica, Inc.™ Used by permission of Zondervan. All rights reserved worldwide. www.zondervan.com The "NIV" and "New International Version" are trademarks registered in the United States Patent and Trademark Office by Biblica, Inc.™

Word First
WOMEN

Made in the USA
Monee, IL
17 March 2020